SAFARI JOKES

Library of Congress Catalog-in-Publication Data
Woodworth, Viki
Jungle/safari jokes / Written and illustrated by Viki Woodworth.
p. cm.
Summary: A collection of riddles featuring jungle animals.
Example: What did the girl lion say to the boy lion? You're my mane man.
ISBN 1-56766-062-2
1. Riddles, Juvenile 2. Jungles–Juvenile humor. 3. Safaris–Juvenile humor.
[1. Jungle animals–Wit and humor 2. Riddles 3. Jokes.]
I. Title.
PN6371.5.W656 1994   92-38581
818.5402–dc20   CIP/AC

SAFARI JOKES

Compiled and Illustrated by
Viki Woodworth

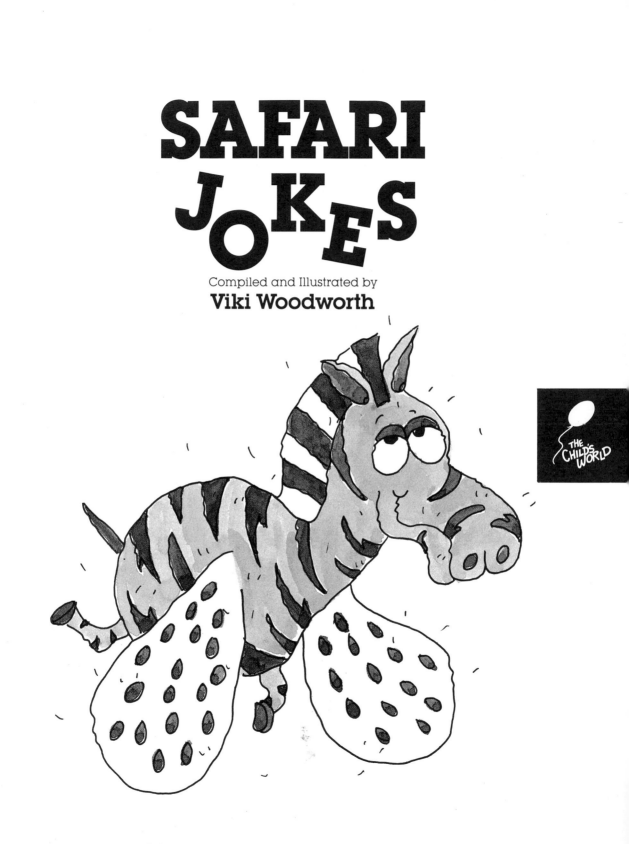

THE CHILD'S WORLD

What is a gorilla's favorite snack?
Potato chimps.

What's worse than a centipede with corns?
A giraffe with a sore throat.

James: Why does a giraffe have a long neck?
Aaron: Because his head is a long way from his body.

What's white on the outside, green on the inside and hops?
A frog sandwich.

Why didn't the frog get his mail?
He forgot his Zip Toad.

What kind of jungle frog is biggest and meanest?
The bully frog.

Nora: Why did the baby snake cry?
Charlotte: Because it lost it's rattle.

What kind of snake tells on other snakes?
A tattle-snake.

What kind of snake is good in a canoe?
A paddle-snake.

Charlotte: What kind of snake loves dessert?
Nora: Pie-thons.

What kind of snake says goodbye a lot?
Bye-thons.

What kind of snake wears sandals?
Py-thongs.

What is red with black stripes?
A sunburned zebra.

How do you see tiny antelopes?
With an ante-scope.

Jenny: What do you call an antelope's mother's brother?
Alison: An uncle-lope.

Which animal refuses to do anything?
The ante-nope.

Which animal can't do anything?
The can't-elope.

Which animal says, "I just can't take it any more!"
The I can't-e-cope.

Which animal doesn't tell the truth?
The lie-on.

What did the girl lion say to the boy lion?
You're my mane man.

What kind of snake is good on a horse?
A saddle-snake.

What is brown on the outside, yellow on the inside and roars?
A lion whole wheat sandwich.

Anna: Does it hurt when a lion gets a haircut?
April: No, it's a painless maneless.

How do you turn off electric lions?
Use it's mane switch.

What do you call a male panther?
Peter: A pant-him.

Which animal is out of shape?
A pant-her.

Which leopard is well trained and protects your house?
A German leopard.

Peter: Why don't leopards ever escape from zoos?
Chris: They're always spotted.

What do leopards like to eat?
Whatever hits the spot.

Which leopard has a lot of energy?
A pep-ard.

What striped animal was born in September?
A Libra zebra.

Which zebras love honey?
The bee-bras.

What animal do comedians love?
The hyena. It laughs at anything.

What do you call a hyena who can't stand up straight?
A hy-lean-a.

Why did the hyena cry when a hippo sat on it?
Because the hyena's funny bone was broken.

Which animal is the laziest?
The loafing hyena.

What instrument does a European rhino play?
The French horn.

What does a rhino do in a traffic jam?
Honks its horn.

What do elephants and trees have in common?
Trunks.

Emily: What do rhinos have that no other animal has?
Trisha: Baby rhinos.

Why do rhinos wear bandaids?
Because they're rhino-sore-aus.

Which rhino is never invited to a party?
The rhino-bore-aus.

John: Why do elephants wear pink sneakers?

Mike: Because their red ones are dirty.

How long are an elephant's legs?

Long enough to reach the ground.

Mike: Why did the elephant sleep with a banana peel?

John: To slip out of bed the next morning.

Which side of an elephant has the most wrinkles?

The outside.

What do you call a rhino with a toad on his back?

A horned toad.

What should you do with a blue elephant?
Cheer it up.

Maria: What is gray, has four legs and a trunk?

Sarah: A mouse on vacation.

Why do elephants paint their toenails green?

So they can hide in the grass.

Sarah: What's wrinkled and gray and lights up?

Maria: An electric elephant?

What's wrinkled and gray and wears glass slippers?

Cinderelephant.

Why did the elephant put the peanut in his trunk?

Because he didn't have a glove compartment.

How do elephants call each other?
On ele-phones

How do monkeys spread gossip?
Through the apevine.

Brandon: What did the gorilla have for dessert?
Eric: Chocolate chimp cookies.

When did the gorilla make a monkey out of himself?
When he went ape over the chimp.

Eric: Why doesn't King Kong eat houses?
Brandon: He's afraid he'll get homesick.

How does an ape open a door?
With a mon-key.

What do you call a flying monkey?
A hot air baboon.